www.raintreepublishers.co.uk
Visit our website to find out
more information about
Raintree books.

To order:

☎ Phone 0845 6044371
🖷 Fax +44 (0) 1865 312263
✉ Email myorders@raintreepublishers.co.uk

Customers from outside the UK please telephone +44 1865 312262

Raintree is an imprint of Capstone Global Library Limited,
a company incorporated in England and Wales having its
registered office at 7 Pilgrim Street, London, EC4V 6LB
– Registered company number: 6695582

Edited by Daniel Nunn, Rebecca Rissman, and Sian Smith
Designed by Cynthia Della-Rovere
Picture research by Mica Brancic
Production by Victoria Fitzgerald
Originated by Capstone Global Library Ltd
Printed and bound in China by South China Printing
Company Ltd

ISBN 978 1 406 23906 5
16 15 14 13 12
10 9 8 7 6 5 4 3 2 1

British Library Cataloguing in Publication Data
Nunn, Daniel.
Numbers in German. -- (World languages. Numbers)
438.2'421-dc23
A full catalogue record for this book is available from the British Library.

Acknowledgements
We would like to thank Shutterstock for permission to reproduce
photographs: © Agorohov, © Aleksandrs Poliscuks, © Alex James Bramwell,
© Andreas Gradin, © Andrey Armyagov, © archidea, © Arogant, © atoss,
© Baloncici, © Benjamin Mercer, © blackpixel, © charles taylor, © Chris
Bradshaw, © cloki, © dcwcreations, © DenisNata, © Diana Taliun, © Eric
Isselée, © Erik Lam, © Fatseyeva, © Feng Yu, © g215, © Hywit Dimyadi, ©
Iv Nikolny, © J. Waldron, © jgl247, © joingate, © karam Miri, © Karkas, ©
kedrov, © LittleMiss, © Ljupco Smokovski, © Lori Sparkia, © Max Krasnov,
© Michelangelus, © Mike Flippo, © mimo, © Nordling, © Olga Popova,
© Pavel Sazonov, © pics fine, © Rosery, © Ruth Black, © Shmel, © Stacy
Barnett, © Steve Collender, © Suzanna, © Tania Zbrodko, © topseller, ©
Vasina Natalia, © Veniamin Kraskov, © Vinicius Tupinamba, © Volodymyr
Krasyuk, © Vorm in Beeld, © Winston Link, © xpixel.

Cover photographs reproduced with permission of Shutterstock: number
1 (© Leigh Prather), number 2 (© Glovatskiy), number 3 (© Phuriphat).
Back cover photographs of cushions reproduced with permission of
Shutterstock (© Karkas, © karam Miri, © Baloncici).

We would like to thank Regina Irwin and Robert Irwin for their invaluable
assistance in the preparation of this book.

Every effort has been made to contact copyright holders of material
reproduced in this book. Any omissions will be rectified in subsequent
printings if notice is given to the publisher.

Contents

Eins

ein Hund

Hier ist ein Hund.

There is one dog.

ein Pullover

Hier ist ein Pullover.

There is one jumper.

Zwei

eine Katze

Hier sind zwei Katzen.

There are two cats.

ein Schuh

Hier sind zwei Schuhe.

There are two shoes.

Drei

ein Mädchen

Hier sind drei Mädchen.

There are three girls.

ein Stuhl

Hier sind drei Stühle.

There are three chairs.

Vier

ein Vogel

Hier sind vier Vögel.

There are four birds.

ein Kissen

Hier sind vier Kissen.

There are four cushions.

Fünf

ein Spielzeug

Hier sind **fünf** Spielzeuge.

There are five toys.

ein Buch

Hier sind fünf Bücher.

There are five books.

Sechs

ein Mantel

Hier sind sechs Mäntel.

There are six coats.

ein Bleistift

Hier sind sechs Bleistifte.

There are six pencils.

Sieben

eine Orange

Hier sind sieben Orangen.

There are seven oranges.

ein Keks

Hier sind sieben Kekse.

There are seven biscuits.

Acht

ein Auto

Hier sind acht Autos.

There are eight cars.

ein Hut

Hier sind acht Hüte.

There are eight hats.

Neun

ein Luftballon

Hier sind neun Luftballons.

There are nine balloons.

eine Kerze

Hier sind neun Kerzen.

There are nine candles.

Zehn

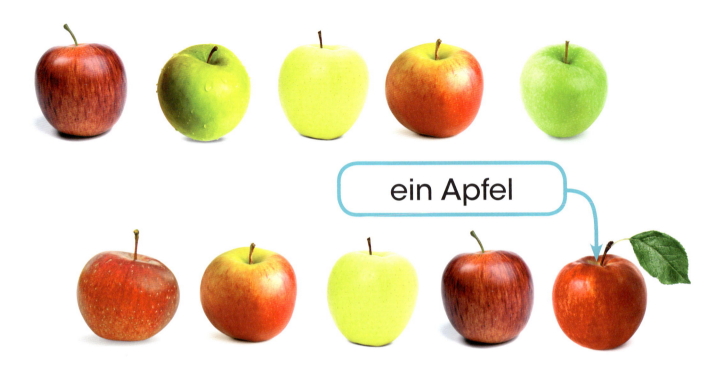

ein Apfel

Hier sind zehn Äpfel.

There are ten apples.

eine Blume

Hier sind zehn Blumen.

There are ten flowers.

Dictionary

See words in the "How to say it" columns for a rough guide to pronunciations.

German word	How to say it	English word
acht	a-ch-t*	eight
Apfel / Äpfel	ap-foll / aip-fall	apple / apples
Auto / Autos	au-toe / au-toes	car / cars
Bleistift / Bleistifte	bleye-steeft / bleye-steeftah	pencil / pencils
Blume / Blumen	bloom-ah / bloomen	flower / flowers
Buch / Bücher	booch / bewcher*	book / books
drei	dry	three
ein / eine	eye-n / eye-nah	a / an
eins	eye-ns	one
fünf	foon-f	five
hier ist / hier sind	hear ist / hear sinned	here is / here are, or there is / there are
Hund	hoont	dog
Hut / Hüte	hoot / hew-tah	hat / hats
Katze / Katzen	cat-zah / cat-zen	cat / cats
Keks / Kekse	cake-ss / cake-ssah	biscuit / biscuits
Kerze / Kerzen	ker-tzah / ker-tzen	candle / candles

22

*Note: In this word "ch" sounds roughly like the "ch" in the Scottish word "loch".

German word	How to say it	English word
Kissen	kiss-en	cushion / cushions
Luftballon / Luftballons	looft-ballon / looft-ballons	balloon / balloons
Mädchen	made-chen*	girl / girls
Mantel / Mäntel	man-tall / men-tell	coat / coats
neun	noin	nine
Orange / Orangen	o-rangah / o-rangen	orange / oranges
Pullover	pull-over	jumper
Schuh / Schuhe	shoo / shoo-ah	shoe / shoes
sechs	seks	six
sieben	sea-ben	seven
Spielzeug / Spielzeuge	speel-tzoig / speel-tzoig-ah	toy / toys
Stuhl / Stühle	stool / stew-le	chair / chairs
vier	fear	four
Vogel / Vögel	fo-guel / fur-guel	bird / birds
zehn	tze-an	ten
zwei	tz-why	two

*Note: In this word "ch" sounds roughly like the "ch" in the Scottish word "loch".

Index

Notes for parents and teachers

In German, nouns always begin with a capital letter. The phrases "There is" and "There are" are not used in German in this context, so we have used the construction "Hier ist" and "Hier sind" ("Here is" and "Here are") instead. The spelling of the German word for "a" or "an" changes depending on how it is used in a sentence – either "ein", "eine" or "einen". "Eins" is used when you write the number one as a numeral.